Learn by Handwriting

Practice Workbook

Cursive 2

Numbers from 1 to 50

Numbers and Words

Our Advantage

Numbers from 1 to 50 - Numbers and Words - Cursive 2
Memorescribe Learn by Handwriting Practice Workbook
Copyright © 2024 by Globaloft, LLC
Alpharetta, GA

Publishing Credits | Authors, Editors, Interior & Cover Designers: Jessica Cobo and Victor Cobo

Memorescribe Product # N150C2PE

TABLE OF CONTENTS

Dearest Persevering Writer,

One of my proudest achievements at the age of 8 was learning to read and write in cursive. Learning cursive whisked me away on adventures as I read my grandparents' beautiful handwritten travel postcards. Even today, I cherish my grandmother's handwritten recipe card as well as her personalized book inscriptions that I have the chance to re-read as I pass those books along to my children.

Many of us can remember the time before handwriting was eclipsed by digital communication. Consider the present reality, all the text messages and emails we read but barely remember and rarely keep as a treasured memory. While there are innumerable benefits to computer use and digital communication, handwriting remains a powerful, valuable skill.

Memorescribe Learn by Handwriting workbooks began as a passion project. When working to help my child develop handwriting skills, I discovered an opportunity to use handwriting practice time to learn and reinforce important educational information. Memorescribe workbooks offer you the opportunity to practice and develop your personal, unique handwriting style while taking advantage of the time to learn something new or reinforce information you learned in the past.

Wherever you are on your journey, no matter your age or handwriting ability, my hope is that Memorescribe's Learn by Handwriting workbooks will send you off on your own learning adventures, travelling as far as your handwriting will take you.

Jessica

Welcome to Memorescribe

Memorescribe Learn by Handwriting workbooks create a fun and meaningful opportunity to commit educational information to memory while you practice your handwriting because we believe handwriting is an invaluable skill. **Learn as you write with Memorescribe!**

IMPORTANCE OF HANDWRITING

1. Writing by hand is a **foundational educational skill** connected to academic progress and success.

2. Writing by hand **activates** different parts of **the brain** and can **boost** your **brain function**.

3. Writing by hand helps to **develop** the **small movements** and **coordination skills** needed for **success in everyday life**.

4. Handwriting notes helps to **organize thoughts** and **process information** more **deeply** which can lead to **better learning**, understanding, **retaining**, and recalling **information**.

5. A unique form of personal expression, handwriting can **display individual personality**, creative tendencies, and artistic craftsmanship as well as **verify identity**.

6. Writing by hand can help to **process emotions, set goals,** soothe and calm while encouraging **personal reflection** on experiences and circumstances.

7. Handwritten notes and documents convey a **memorable,** meaningful, **personal touch** and **demonstrate care** and thoughtfulness towards the recipient.

8. Preserving methods and styles of handwriting allows people groups and cultures the opportunity to **maintain heritage** and **safeguard history**.

Print and Cursive Handwriting

Print Handwriting, also known as Manuscript, is patterned after the style of letters commonly used in printed materials such as books, newspapers, or magazines. Each letter is written independently and is not connected to any other letter. To create print style handwriting, the writer lifts the pen or pencil from the paper after forming each letter. Print handwriting is simple and can often be easier to read than cursive style writing.

Cursive Handwriting is also known as Script, longhand, or joined-up writing. The scripted style of writing is created using connected, flowing letters which allows for faster, more elegant writing than print. Writers of cursive use single strokes to create letters without lifting the pen or pencil from the paper and connect the letters within the same word. Cursive handwriting is more intricate than print and can add a touch of sophistication whenever used.

With **Memorescribe, you can choose your handwriting style and text size.** For handwriting style, choose between print and cursive. For handwriting text size, choose from level 1, level 2, or level 3 in your selected style.

Workbooks are available in the following style and size options:

Books available in English, Spanish, and other languages.

Recommendations for Comfortable Handwriting

Pencil Grip Tip:

Pinch the pencil between your thumb and first finger. Rest the pinched fingers with pencil on the middle finger. Curl the last two fingers into the palm of your hand for support as you rest your hand on the writing surface.

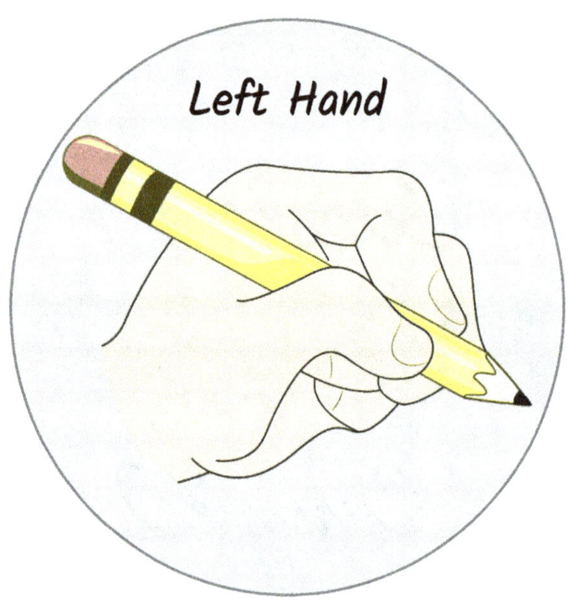

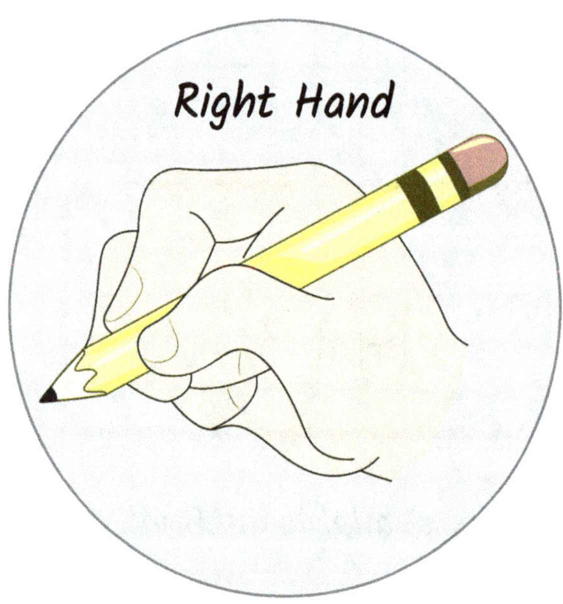

Supportive Handwriting Pencil Grip

PRACTICE MAKES THE MASTER

Numbers from 1 to 50

1 One	11 Eleven	21 Twenty-one	31 Thirty-one	41 Forty-one
2 Two	12 Twelve	22 Twenty-two	32 Thirty-two	42 Forty-two
3 Three	13 Thirteen	23 Twenty-three	33 Thirty-three	43 Forty-three
4 Four	14 Fourteen	24 Twenty-four	34 Thirty-four	44 Forty-four
5 Five	15 Fifteen	25 Twenty-five	35 Thirty-five	45 Forty-five
6 Six	16 Sixteen	26 Twenty-six	36 Thirty-six	46 Forty-six
7 Seven	17 Seventeen	27 Twenty-seven	37 Thirty-seven	47 Forty-seven
8 Eight	18 Eighteen	28 Twenty-eight	38 Thirty-eight	48 Forty-eight
9 Nine	19 Nineteen	29 Twenty-nine	39 Thirty-nine	49 Forty-nine
10 Ten	20 Twenty	30 Thirty	40 Forty	50 Fifty

Numbers and Words

1 One   -   2 Two   -   3 Three

1 One - 2 Two - 3 Three

4 Four – 5 Five – 6 Six

4 Four - 5 Five - 6 Six

7 Seven   -   8 Eight   -   9 Nine

memorescribe.com

Numbers 1 to 50

© Globaloft, LLC

7 Seven — 8 Eight — 9 Nine

10 Ten — 11 Eleven — 12 Twelve

10 Ten   -   11 Eleven   -   12 Twelve

13 Thirteen   —   14 Fourteen

1

2

3

4

5

6

7

8

9

10

11

12

13

13 Thirteen   —   14 Fourteen

15 Fifteen – 16 Sixteen

15 Fifteen — 16 Sixteen

17 Seventeen   -   18 Eighteen

1

2

3

4

5

6

7

8

9

10

11

12

13

17 Seventeen — 18 Eighteen

Numbers 1 to 50

memorescribe.com

19 Nineteen   –   20 Twenty

memorescribe.com

Numbers 1 to 50

© Globaloft, LLC

19 Nineteen — 20 Twenty

21 Twenty-one – 22 Twenty-two

21 Twenty-one – 22 Twenty-two

Numbers 1 to 50

memorescribe.com

23 Twenty-three

23 Twenty-three

24 Twenty-four

24 Twenty-four

Break Activity 1
Word Search

Directions:


```
Y  P  K  B  T  O  X  M  T  D  J  A  J  V
S  E  V  E  N  H  Q  H  W  U  I  P  I  S
G  D  T  D  E  Q  I  Y  E  Y  Y  V  O  L
N  W  P  H  E  R  M  R  N  V  T  S  Y  G
C  G  A  X  T  P  R  T  T  M  L  F  V  M
Q  L  H  Y  E  Q  H  B  Y  E  P  E  I  R
H  D  S  V  N  G  A  I  O  W  E  W  W  F
T  I  V  M  I  E  R  M  N  Y  U  N  E  T
X  O  S  E  N  H  T  A  E  K  E  X  P  I
I  Z  J  A  R  E  V  I  F  Y  T  R  O  F
V  T  H  I  R  T  Y  N  I  N  E  B  P  S
R  U  O  F  Y  T  R  O  F  Z  Y  M  F  S
S  O  J  T  W  E  N  T  Y  T  H  R  E  E
W  D  O  E  P  F  N  Y  L  D  V  N  L  E
```

EIGHT	FIFTY	FORTY-FIVE	FORTY-FOUR
NINETEEN	SEVEN	THIRTEEN	THIRTY-NINE
THIRTY-SIX	TWELVE	TWENTY-ONE	TWENTY-THREE

Break Activity 2
Crossword

Directions: *Use the clues below to discover the missing words. Words share letters where they cross in the puzzle.*

ACROSS

4. The number of days in the month of December

5. The number of fingers on one hand

6. The number of eyes in a group of ten people

7. The number of eggs in three dozen

DOWN

1. The number of hours in two days

2. The number of months in a year

3. The number of wheels in a pair of roller skates

25 Twenty-five

1

2

3

4

5

6

7

8

9

10

11

12

13

25 Twenty-five

35

26 Twenty-six

26 Twenty-six

27 Twenty-seven

1

2

3

4

5

6

7

8

9

10

11

12

13

27 Twenty-seven

28 Twenty-eight

28 Twenty-eight

29 Twenty-nine - 30 Thirty

1

2

3

4

5

6

7

8

9

10

11

12

13

29 Twenty-nine – 30 Thirty

Numbers 1 to 50

memorescribe.com

31 Thirty-one - 32 Thirty-two

1

2

3

4

5

6

7

8

9

10

11

12

13

31 Thirty-one — 32 Thirty-two

33 Thirty-three – 34 Thirty-four

33 Thirty-three — 34 Thirty-four

Numbers 1 to 50

memorescribe.com

35 Thirty-five - 36 Thirty-six

35 Thirty-five   -   36 Thirty-six

37 Thirty-seven – 38 Thirty-eight

37 Thirty-seven – 38 Thirty-eight

39 Thirty-nine   -   40 Forty

39 Thirty-nine   —   40 Forty

41 Forty-one - 42 Forty-two

memorescribe.com

Numbers 1 to 50

© Globaloft, LLC

41 Forty-one - 42 Forty-two

43 Forty-three - 44 Forty-four

43 Forty-three – 44 Forty-four

45 Forty-five - 46 Forty-six

45 Forty-five - 46 Forty-six

47 Forty-seven – 48 Forty-eight

Numbers from 1 to 50

47 Forty-seven – 48 Forty-eight

49 Forty-nine   -   50 Fifty

49 Forty-nine   -   50 Fifty

Directions:

Search to find the list of words hidden inside the puzzle. Words can go in any direction and can share letters.

```
W  E  C  A  X  T  Q  Y  Y  I  B  Y  W  L
W  I  N  U  W  V  B  B  J  F  H  Q  N  T
K  G  H  E  S  I  X  T  E  E  N  F  L  P
N  H  N  R  V  Y  V  W  S  L  X  U  X  E
V  T  U  R  T  E  W  C  E  I  X  C  V  K
Y  E  Z  N  U  W  S  B  W  Y  G  I  U  S
J  E  K  E  S  O  E  Y  Z  H  F  P  D  J
N  N  K  B  L  C  F  N  T  Y  W  P  T  D
E  U  E  E  R  H  T  Y  T  R  I  H  T  T
T  X  L  R  V  M  A  R  T  Y  O  O  G  H
F  O  R  T  Y  N  I  N  E  N  T  F  N  R
D  J  W  L  E  H  H  E  H  D  E  W  H  E
I  A  Y  R  T  O  K  Z  E  Y  F  W  O  E
V  T  H  G  I  E  Y  T  R  I  H  T  T  V
```

EIGHTEEN	FORTY-NINE	FORTY-SEVEN	SIXTEEN
TEN	THIRTY-EIGHT	THIRTY-FIVE	THIRTY-THREE
THREE	TWENTY	TWENTY-FOUR	TWENTY-TWO

Break Activity 4
Crossword

Directions: Use the clues below to discover the missing words. Words share letters where they cross in the puzzle.

ACROSS

3. The number of toes on both feet combined

4. The number of days in five weeks

5. Half the number of weeks of the year

6. The number of letters in the name of the first month of the year

DOWN

1. The number half way between 0 and 30

2. The number half way between 40 and 50

Break Activities Solutions

Break Activity 1 - Page 32: **Word Search**

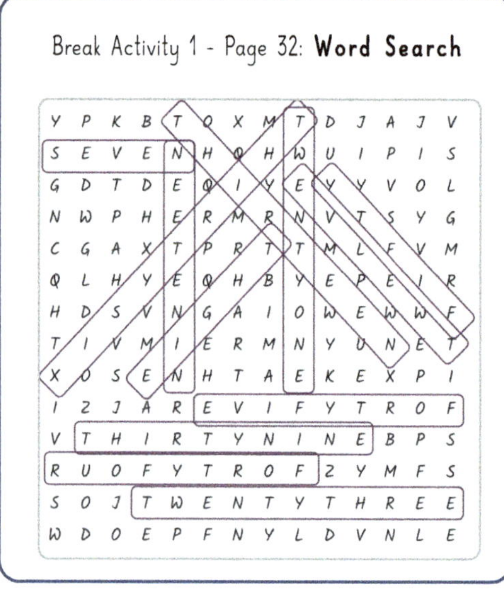

Break Activity 3 - Page 64: **Word Search**

Break Activity 2 - Page 33: **Crossword**

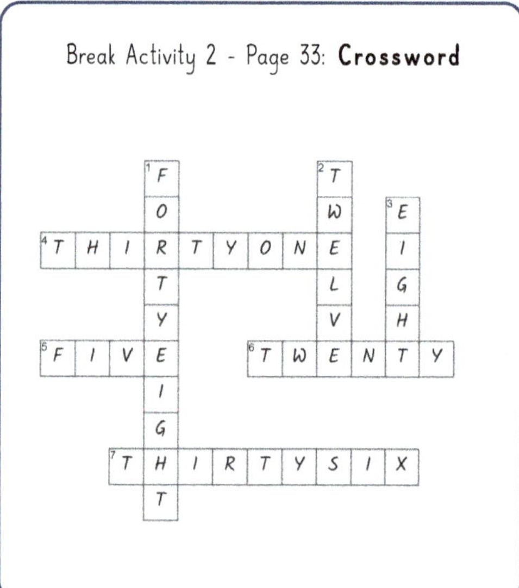

Break Activity 4 - Page 65: **Crossword**

Memorescribe Workbook Themes

Family

Nature

Math

Manners

Faith

Science

World

Sports

General Knowledge

and more to come!

Contact us for customized content for your organization or project.

www.ingramcontent.com/pod-product-compliance
Lightning Source LLC
Chambersburg PA
CBHW081406130726
47998CB00011B/3093